Seabirds

Published by Wildlife Education, Ltd.
9820 Willow Creek Road, Suite 300, San Diego, California 92131

ISBN 0-937934-90-9

Seabirds

Series Created by
John Bonnett Wexo

Written by
Beth Wagner Brust

Zoological Consultant
Charles R. Schroeder, D.V.M.
Director Emeritus
San Diego Zoo and San Diego Wild Animal Park

Scientific Consultant
Frank S. Todd
EcoCepts International

Art Credits

Paintings: Tim Hayward
Activities Art: Elizabeth Morales-Denney

Photographic Credits

Front Cover: Frans Lanting *(Photo Researchers, Inc.)*

Page Eight: Helen Williams *(Photo Researchers, Inc.)*

Page Nine: Gregory G. Dimijian *(Photo Researchers, Inc.)*

Page Ten: G. Ziesler *(Bruce Coleman, Ltd.)*

Page Eleven: Upper Middle, Jeff Simon *(Bruce Coleman, Ltd.)*; **Lower Middle**, G.L. Kooyman *(Animals Animals)*

Page Twelve: Left, Tom Mangelsen *(Images of Nature)*; **Lower Right**, Yoichi R. Okamoto *(Photo Researchers, Inc.)*

Pages Fourteen and Fifteen: George H. Balazs

Page Sixteen: Frans Lanting *(Minden Pictures)*

Page Seventeen: Middle Right, Cristina Smith *(Wildlife Education, Ltd.)*; **Lower Right**, David Madison *(Bruce Coleman, Inc.)*

Page Eighteen: Anthony Bannister *(NHPA)*

Page Nineteen: Frans Lanting *(Photo Researchers, Inc.)*

Page Twenty: Middle Left, Gilbert S. Grant *(Photo Researchers, Inc.)*; **Lower Left**, Charles Feil

Page Twenty-One: Gerald Cubitt *(Bruce Coleman, Ltd.)*

Page Twenty-Two: Upper Left, Frans Lanting *(Minden Pictures)*; **Lower Left**: Cristina Smith *(Wildlife Education, Ltd.)*

Page Twenty-Three: Marty Knapp *(Wildlife Education, Ltd.)*

Our Thanks To: Alan Lieberman *(Zoological Society of San Diego)*; Kimball Garrett, Ph.D. *(Los Angeles County Museum of Natural History)*; Frank Twohy *(Sea World)*; Wendy Perkins *(San Diego Zoo Library)*; Pepe Gonzalez; Paul Brust; Joe Selig

Cover Photo: Laysan albatross

Contents

WANDERING ALBATROSS
Diomedea exulans

Seabirds are simply amazing. Some can soar through the air without ever flapping their wings. Others are as at home in the water as they are in the air. And still others can't fly at all.

Of the 260 or more seabird species, gulls are among the most widely distributed. They live along the coasts of every continent of the world. And they tend to gather in cities and in other places where people are— at beaches, in harbors, and along coastal waterways. This has made gulls the best known of all seabirds.

But now you're about to discover many other types of seabirds as well, some that you may not have seen before —like the graceful albatross and the pesky frigatebird. And you'll begin to understand why seabirds are an endless source of fascination for people everywhere.

The wandering albatross is the world's largest seabird. It has a wingspan of over 11 feet (3.35 meters). And it weighs more than 20 pounds (9 kilograms).

PARASITIC JAEGAR
Stercorarius parasiticus

BROWN PELICAN
Pelecanus occidentalis

NORTHERN FULMAR
Fulmarus glacialis

COMMON MURRE
Uria aalge

WILSON'S STORM PETREL
Oceanites oceanicus

RED-NECKED PHALAROPE
Phalaropus lobatus

The smallest seabirds are the tiny storm petrels. They can weigh as little as 14 grams (½ ounce)! And their bodies are only 5 to 9 inches long (13 to 23 centimeters)!

ATLANTIC PUFFIN
Fratercula arctic

EUROPEAN EIDER DUCK
Somateria mollissima mollissima

HERRING GULL
Larus argentatus

MAGNIFICENT FRIGATEBIRD
Fregata magnificens

The frigatebird, shown at right, is the most agile of all seabirds! It can swoop, dart, soar, and hover better than any other seabird. You can always tell a male frigate by the bright red throat pouch that it displays during the mating season.

STELLER'S SEA EAGLE
Haliaeetus pelagicus

RED-BILLED TROPICBIRD
Phaethon aethereus

ARCTIC TERN
Sterna paradisaea

BROWN BOOBY
Sula leucogaster

A seabird is any bird that spends most of its time at sea. Seabirds that spend almost *all* of their time on the open sea are called *pelagic* (peh-LAJ-ick) seabirds. These birds generally come ashore only to breed and raise their young.

BLACK SKIMMER
Rynchops niger

CORMORANT
Phalacrocorax sp.

GALAPAGOS PENGUIN
Spheniscus mendiculus

Penguins cannot fly, but they can swim and dive better than any other bird in the world. Some species can dive as deep as 870 feet (265 meters)!

7

The bodies of large seabirds are built for flying. That's because flying is their key to survival. They fly to find food. They fly to escape danger. And they fly to their nesting sites to lay eggs and raise their young. Some large seabirds spend so much time flying that they have lost the ability to walk or swim. These birds, which can be so graceful in the air, are often clumsy on land.

One thing that helps large seabirds fly so well is that their bodies are quite small in relation to their wings. The lighter a bird's body and the larger its wings, the easier it is to lift off the ground and soar. Some large seabirds can fly without even flapping their wings!

But as you will see on these pages, large seabirds are built for more than just flying. They also have special features that help them catch food, keep themselves clean, and stay warm in their cold ocean habitat.

Frigatebirds are masters of flight. They can eat *and even sleep* while flying! It's hard to believe that such graceful fliers can hardly walk or swim. But it's true—a frigate's feet are too small for it to move well on land. And its feathers are not waterproof, so it seldom lands on water.

A seabird's beak is designed for the type of food it eats. The long, narrow beak of this gannet, for example, is perfect for catching and holding slippery fish.

The short, rounded beak of this little auk helps it scoop up tiny animals, called zooplankton, that float through the ocean.

The slightly hooked beak of the herring gull helps it catch and eat a wide variety of foods —including fish, eggs, garbage, other birds, and anything else it can find.

The skimmer is the only bird in the world whose *lower* bill is much longer than its *upper* bill. The long lower bill enables the skimmer to pick up food as it skims along the ocean's surface. When the lower bill strikes a fish, the upper bill snaps down and grabs it.

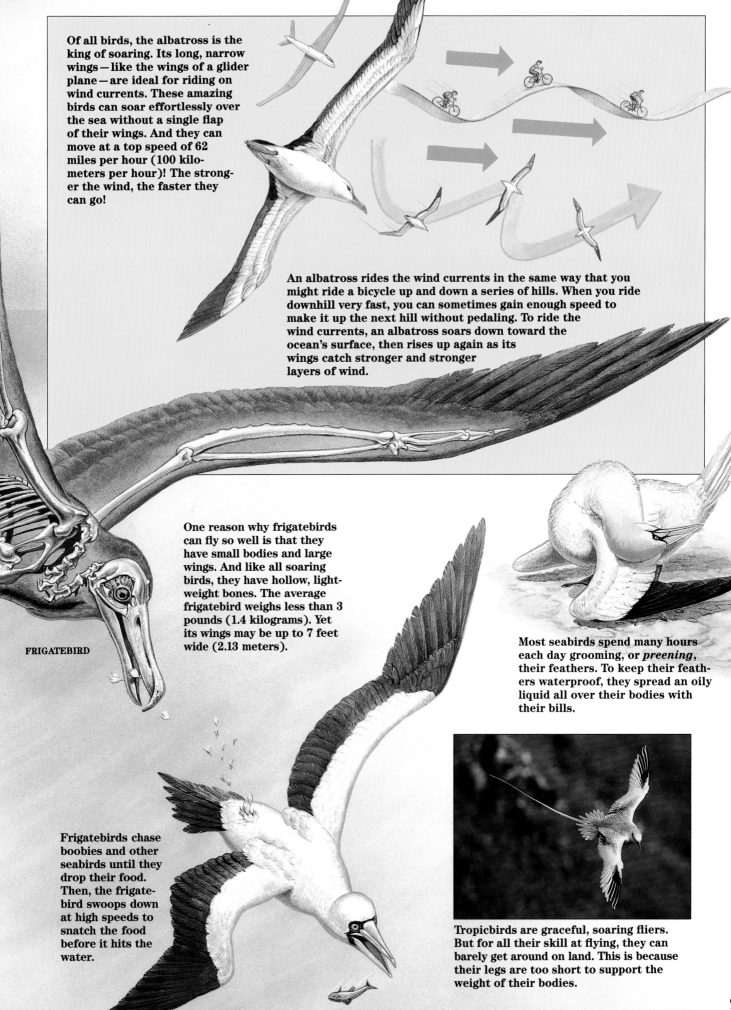

Of all birds, the albatross is the king of soaring. Its long, narrow wings—like the wings of a glider plane—are ideal for riding on wind currents. These amazing birds can soar effortlessly over the sea without a single flap of their wings. And they can move at a top speed of 62 miles per hour (100 kilometers per hour)! The stronger the wind, the faster they can go!

An albatross rides the wind currents in the same way that you might ride a bicycle up and down a series of hills. When you ride downhill very fast, you can sometimes gain enough speed to make it up the next hill without pedaling. To ride the wind currents, an albatross soars down toward the ocean's surface, then rises up again as its wings catch stronger and stronger layers of wind.

One reason why frigatebirds can fly so well is that they have small bodies and large wings. And like all soaring birds, they have hollow, lightweight bones. The average frigatebird weighs less than 3 pounds (1.4 kilograms). Yet its wings may be up to 7 feet wide (2.13 meters).

FRIGATEBIRD

Most seabirds spend many hours each day grooming, or *preening*, their feathers. To keep their feathers waterproof, they spread an oily liquid all over their bodies with their bills.

Frigatebirds chase boobies and other seabirds until they drop their food. Then, the frigatebird swoops down at high speeds to snatch the food before it hits the water.

Tropicbirds are graceful, soaring fliers. But for all their skill at flying, they can barely get around on land. This is because their legs are too short to support the weight of their bodies.

The bodies of diving seabirds are designed for life in the water. Most seabirds can swim on the *surface*, paddling with their webbed feet. But diving seabirds can also swim *under* the water.

Diving seabirds have special features to help them survive in the ocean. For example, their legs are set farther back on their bodies than are those of other seabirds. This helps them move faster and steer better when they dive.

And many diving seabirds use more than their feet to swim. Puffins and diving petrels use their wings like paddles. They "fly" underwater in much the same way that they fly through the air!

Diving petrels are excellent underwater fliers. Small flocks of these birds will soar up to a wave before it breaks and plunge right through it—popping out on the other side without missing a wingbeat!

Some diving seabirds, like this cormorant, use their webbed feet to help them swim underwater. They make themselves streamlined by flattening their wings against their bodies.

Other divers, like puffins, are also underwater fliers. They beat their wings up and down to chase after fast fish. And they use their feet to steer!

Puffins have spines on their tongues and on the roofs of their mouths. These spines help them catch and hold slippery fish. They can hold *as many as 60 little fish* at once!

AUK

Seabirds have excellent vision. With one eye on each side of its head, a seabird can spot food or predators *without turning at all!*

A special gland above a seabird's eyes helps it remove salt from its food and water. The salt is removed in a liquid form. It runs down the seabird's beak and drips off the end of its bill.

Auks and penguins look so much alike, you might think they are closely related. But they are actually very different. Auks, which can fly, live in the Arctic. But penguins, which cannot fly, live in and around Antarctica.

PENGUIN

A diving petrel's wings are adapted for both flying and swimming. Underwater, petrels use their short wings like paddles. And in the air, they fly near the water's surface, where it is less windy.

Penguins are champion swimmers and divers. That's because their bodies are the perfect shape for life in the water. They are sleek and streamlined to make swimming easier. And their short wings are stiff and strong to push them through the water.

11

Food is the most important thing in a seabird's life. Favorite foods of seabirds include fish, small shrimp, shellfish, and squid. But finding these foods is not always easy. For this reason, seabirds spend most of their time looking for their next meal.

Some seabirds, including albatrosses, terns, and tropicbirds, spend months—even years—at sea. During this time, they never come ashore. But they do land on the water from time to time to rest. On these pages, you'll learn more about how seabirds find their food. And you'll see how different types of seabirds have developed their own special feeding techniques.

① Brown pelicans, shown at left and below, *plunge dive* to find food. They soar high above the water until they spot a fish below. Then they dive straight down to where the fish is swimming.

ARCTIC TERN

Some seabirds find food by *snatching* it from the ocean's surface. This arctic tern has grabbed a fish from the water and is eating it as it flies away. It takes skillful flying and good eyesight to get a meal this way!

MURRES

Many seabirds *dive* to find their food. These murres (MURRS), for example, take a deep dive from the water's surface and swim long distances under the water to catch a meal.

The red phalarope (FALL-ah-ROPE), a bird that lives in the Arctic, *feeds at the surface* of the water. First, it paddles around in a circle. This creates a swirl, which pulls bits of food up to the surface. Then it pokes its bill into the center to feed.

RED PHALAROPE

See for yourself how a phalarope feeds. Fill a clear mixing bowl with water. Sprinkle bread crumbs onto the surface and wait until they sink. Then put your finger in the water, and swirl it around a few times. The current created by your finger should pull the crumbs up toward the surface.

Some seabirds steal, or *scavenge*, their food from fishermen, from other birds, and even from garbage dumps. Gulls, shown above, are among the most famous of all seabird scavengers.

JAEGER

Jaegers often try to steal food from puffins. When a puffin has fish, it hides within a group of nonfeeding puffins. The jaeger can't tell that it has food, and so it leaves the puffin alone.

PUFFINS

Gulls love to eat clams and other shellfish. And they have a clever way of getting to the meat inside. They simply drop the clam onto the rocks to smash open the shell. Then they swoop down and grab the meat.

② The pelican hits the water at high speed. Then it opens its beak and scoops up the fish in its huge pouch.

When a pelican comes up after a dive, it tips its head to the side to dump the water from its pouch. Frigates may take this opportunity to move in and steal the pelican's catch! They land on the bird's head or beak and then reach into the pouch to grab the fish.

③ A pelican's pouch is so big that it can hold up to 3 gallons of water (11 liters)!

13

Some masked booby chicks, like the one in this picture, grow to be even larger than their parents! This chick still has mostly down feathers. Its flight feathers are just beginning to show.

Seabirds communicate through special signals called *displays*. A display can be a body movement, a sound, or even a physical change—like becoming more colorful. And it can take place in the air, on land, or even under the water.

Seabirds display for many different reasons. They display to attract mates and to show affection. They display to say "hello" to each other or to signal a fight. And they display for some reasons that are unknown to scientists.

The most common seabird displays have to do with mating. Most seabirds mate for life. And males and females both care for the young. For these reasons, seabirds choose their partners carefully. Scientists believe that seabird displays may help partners stay together so that they can rear their young.

Many seabirds come ashore only about once a year to mate. Often, they return to the same spot each year, in groups of thousands, or even *millions*!

When boobies want to attract a mate, they point their bills to the sky. This type of display is called *skypointing*.

To scare off intruders, seabirds sometimes lower their heads and open their wings to make themselves look bigger than they really are. They may also pull up tufts of grass with their beaks, as if to say, "Don't come any closer, or I'll do this to your feathers!"

Never get too close to an albatross's nest! A threatened albatross will spit out a bad-smelling oil from its stomach to drive an intruder away. And that could be as bad as being sprayed by a skunk!

Pelicans have some unusual ways of showing their moods—like turning their pouches inside out! Some scientists think that this is a sign of comfort and well-being.

Tropicbirds, above, display as they fly through the air. High above the ground, mating tropicbirds fly close together, opening and dipping their long streaming tails.

To show someone that you like them, you might give them a gift. When a male tern wants to show his affection, he presents a female with a fish!

Blue-footed boobies display by flashing their bright blue feet. During the mating season, male boobies land with their webbed feet spread wide. It almost looks like they're braking to a stop. And such big blue feet attract their mate's attention!

Common murres sometimes perform their courting displays underwater. Some scientists have observed them swimming side by side, much like synchronized swimmers.

Baby seabirds hatch from eggs, just like land birds. The major difference between seabirds and land birds is that land birds usually nest alone, whereas most seabirds nest in large groups on remote islands. Islands make perfect nesting sites for seabirds because there are few ground predators to disturb them. Also, there is plenty of wind and airspace for easy takeoffs and landings.

Seabirds are excellent parents, feeding and guarding their chicks until they are ready to leave the nest. Cold, heat, predators, and starvation are the most life-threatening things for young chicks. But if they can make it through their first year, they can live as long as 40 or 50 years. The oldest seabird on record is a Laysan albatross that lived to be more than 60 years old!

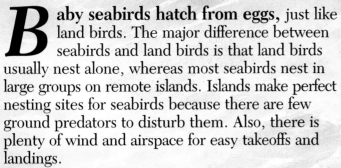

Most seabirds have a small patch of skin, called a *brood patch*, on the lower part of their bellies. They use this patch like an electric blanket to keep their eggs warm until they hatch.

Like most seabirds, gannets live in large groups called *colonies*. Sometimes as many as 500,000 gannets live together in one colony! Living in groups makes it easier for seabirds to alert each other to danger. And when necessary, they can help one another fight off predators.

Puffins use their beaks and feet to carve out tunnels for their nests. Other seabirds use twigs, rocks, or seaweed to make nests. And still others have no nests at all. They lay their eggs on bare rock ledges, on a tree branch, or in a shallow pit of sand.

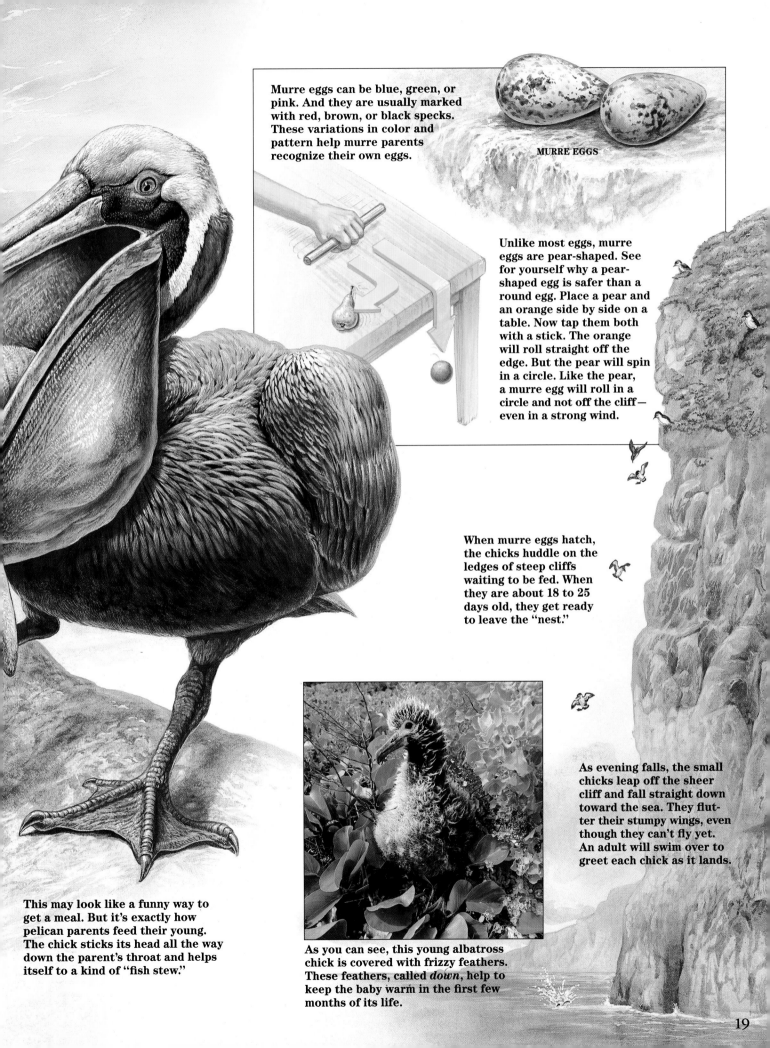

Murre eggs can be blue, green, or pink. And they are usually marked with red, brown, or black specks. These variations in color and pattern help murre parents recognize their own eggs.

MURRE EGGS

Unlike most eggs, murre eggs are pear-shaped. See for yourself why a pear-shaped egg is safer than a round egg. Place a pear and an orange side by side on a table. Now tap them both with a stick. The orange will roll straight off the edge. But the pear will spin in a circle. Like the pear, a murre egg will roll in a circle and not off the cliff—even in a strong wind.

When murre eggs hatch, the chicks huddle on the ledges of steep cliffs waiting to be fed. When they are about 18 to 25 days old, they get ready to leave the "nest."

As evening falls, the small chicks leap off the sheer cliff and fall straight down toward the sea. They flutter their stumpy wings, even though they can't fly yet. An adult will swim over to greet each chick as it lands.

This may look like a funny way to get a meal. But it's exactly how pelican parents feed their young. The chick sticks its head all the way down the parent's throat and helps itself to a kind of "fish stew."

As you can see, this young albatross chick is covered with frizzy feathers. These feathers, called *down*, help to keep the baby warm in the first few months of its life.

19

People have endangered seabirds in many ways. Hungry whalers and fishermen have invaded seabird colonies for eggs and meat. Collectors of exotic feathers have almost caused the extinction of at least one species of seabird. And now the human quest for oil has created a constant threat of ocean pollution. Oil tankers and offshore oil drilling further increase the risk of accidents and spills, which can cause great harm to seabirds and other ocean wildlife.

Fortunately, international laws now protect seabirds. And for most problems created by people, there are solutions. On these pages, you will learn about just a few of the ways that people are trying to help seabirds survive.

More and more people are visiting remote islands where seabirds nest. Such visits can be harmful to the birds that live there. In fact, when people walk through a seabird colony, the birds will take off and leave their nests, their eggs, and even their chicks. If a colony is disturbed more than a few times, the birds will never return to that site again.

In 1844, the last great auk was killed by Icelandic fishermen. Great auks were slow and so they were easy targets for hungry seamen. The only great auks you'll see today are stuffed and in museums, like the one at left.

GREAT AUK

SHORT-TAILED ALBATROSS

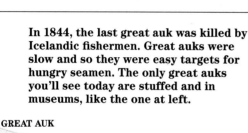

Millions of beautiful short-tailed albatrosses have been killed so that their feathers could be used to stuff mattresses. Today, only about 300 of these birds are left. Only if we protect them will they survive.

Scientists are trying to start puffin colonies in Maine, where huge populations of these birds once lived. First, they place puffin chicks in burrows. Then they surround the burrows with puffin dolls, to look like the chicks' parents. Each day they leave food for the youngsters. When the chicks grow up, they will remember this site and come back to it to raise their own young.

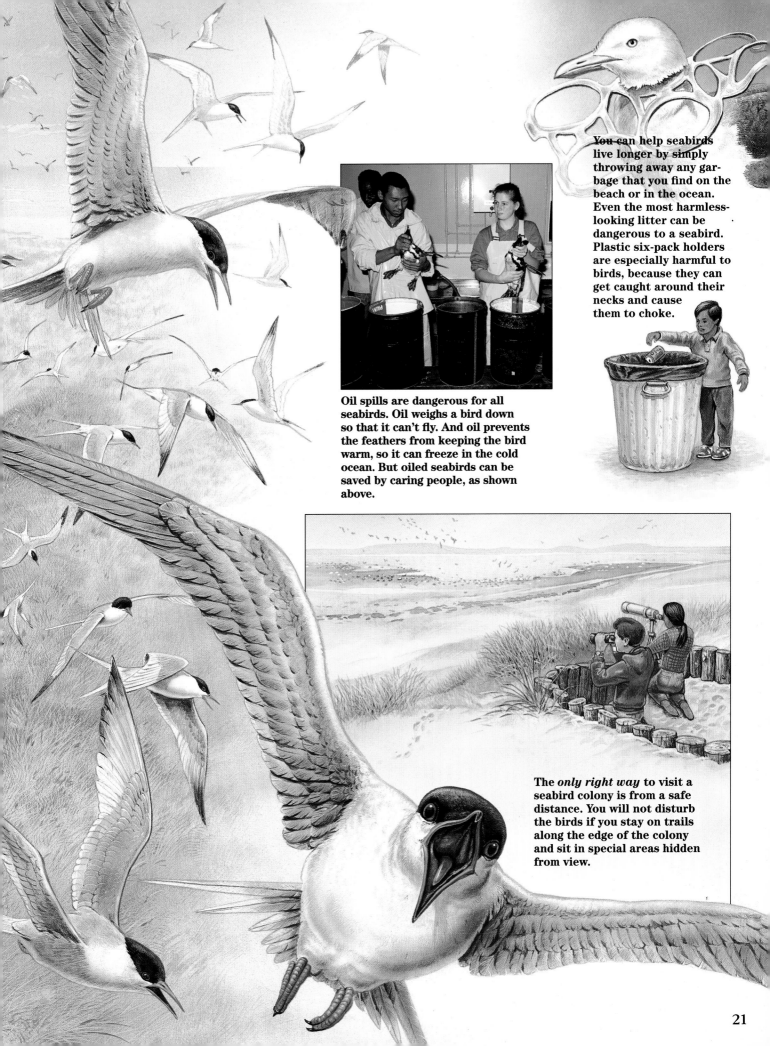

You can help seabirds live longer by simply throwing away any garbage that you find on the beach or in the ocean. Even the most harmless-looking litter can be dangerous to a seabird. Plastic six-pack holders are especially harmful to birds, because they can get caught around their necks and cause them to choke.

Oil spills are dangerous for all seabirds. Oil weighs a bird down so that it can't fly. And oil prevents the feathers from keeping the bird warm, so it can freeze in the cold ocean. But oiled seabirds can be saved by caring people, as shown above.

The *only right way* to visit a seabird colony is from a safe distance. You will not disturb the birds if you stay on trails along the edge of the colony and sit in special areas hidden from view.

21

Dive into these exciting seabird activities. Use what you have learned about seabirds to complete the exercises on these two pages.

Eating Like A Bird

You have read that food is the most important thing in a seabird's life. You have also learned about some of the ways that seabirds find their food. Unscramble the letters in the following words to review five of these feeding methods.

1. PUNGLE VINDIG   2. EPED VIGDIN

3. DEFEGIN TA TEH RUFASEC

4. CATSGHINN OFOD   5. VANGEGCINS

1. Plunge Diving 2. Deep diving
3. Feeding at the surface 4. Snatching food 5. Scavenging

What's Wrong With This Picture?

There are at least ten things wrong in the scene at right. How many of them can you find? What can you do to protect seabirds?

A Picture Perfect Pelican

Study these illustrations to see how you can make your own drawing of a pelican. After you have mastered the art of pelican drawing, try creating a whole colony of pelicans.

A Bill For Every Bird

Beaks are the tools that birds use when they eat. But birds do not all have the same kinds of beaks. This is because they eat different kinds of foods and so they need different kinds of tools to do the job. Study the beaks below. Think about the various seabirds you have read about in this book. Then match each beak below with the seabird it belongs to. If you need to, look back at the pictures on the previous pages.

Gannet   Herring gull   Pelican   Puffin   Skimmer

1.

2.

3.

4.

5.

1. Puffin
2. Pelican
3. Skimmer
4. Herring gull
5. Gannet

Notebook

Large box

Watch The Birdie

Have you ever tried to watch a bird only to have it fly away when it saw you? With a bird blind, you can get a better look at the birds that live in or pass through the area where you live. Be sure to keep notes about what you see. If you have a tape recorder, you might even want to record some of the sounds the birds make.

Holes to look through

Tape recorder

Book to help identify the birds you see

Binoculars

Index